Express Yourself

MY FRIEND, MATILDA

WRITTEN BY BEN KECKLER

ILLUSTRATED BY DICK DAVIS

CREATIVE DEVELOPMENT BY DIANA BARNARD

Eagle Creek Publications
PO Box 781166
Indianapolis, Indiana 46278

The book is for the special creatures we are given who are just as eager to teach us as is **My Friend, Matilda.**

Special thanks to Popcorn, Bowinkle, Snowflake, Gladdie, Cody and Sandie.

--B.K.

My Friend, Matilda
Text copyright © 2006 by Benjamin F. Keckler, III
Illustrations copyright © by Benjamin F. Keckler, III
Printed in the USA
Eagle Creek Publications, PO Box 781166, Indianapolis, Indiana 46278
www.eaglecreekpubs.com

Library of Congress Cataloguing-In-Publication Data
Keckler III, Benjamin F.
  My Friend, Matilda/by Ben Keckler; illustrated by Dick Davis; artistic consultant Diana Barnard; 1st ed.
  p.   cm.
  Summary: A caring pet offers unconditional friendship during every transition in a young man's life.
  ISBN 0-9769093-1-6
  [1.Stories in rhyme 2. Pets, Grief 3.Self-help: Transition, Grief]

This book is dedicated to Christopher Morrison

THIS BOOK IS CREATED ESPECIALLY
FOR YOU BY A WHOLE TEAM OF
PEOPLE WHO WANT YOU TO BE
THE BEST YOU CAN BE.
BEN, CHERYL, DIANA, DICK,
MIKE C. AND MIKE R. ALONG WITH LORI
AND, OF COURSE, MATILDA, HAVE COME
TOGETHER TO BRING YOU THIS SPECIAL
STORY ABOUT CHRIS AND MATILDA'S
LIFE EXPERIENCES.

WE'RE THINKING OF YOU!

Hi! I've got something to tell you,

Might help when you're blue

A story about a dear friend and me,

Loving and faithful to the thousandth degree!

This rhyme I'm sharing is about Matilda, my pet,

Please sit back and listen, you'll have no regret.

She's a golden retriever; at least that's what they say.

She runs and she slobbers and with toys she does play.

Sometimes she's annoying and I have to say, "Get!"

But I like her the best when by my side she does sit.

She's been with me for many, many great years;

She's most loving when I'm drowning in tears!

No matter the problem she'll come and she'll see

If there's anything special she can do just for me.

I've not done much for her affection to earn,

And so, when she bugs me, I never can spurn

To give her attention and play with her some,

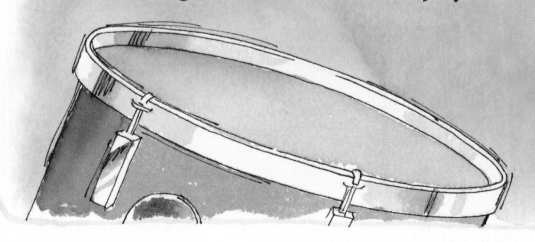

'Cause when I do, her bark becomes mum!

I've got to tell you this story comes with a twist.

It could make you mad and pound with your fist.

It could make you sad and bring a tear to your eye,

Or bring you relief and cause you to sigh.

One day I learned I was really quite sick.

Matilda seemed to know it, by my side she would stick.

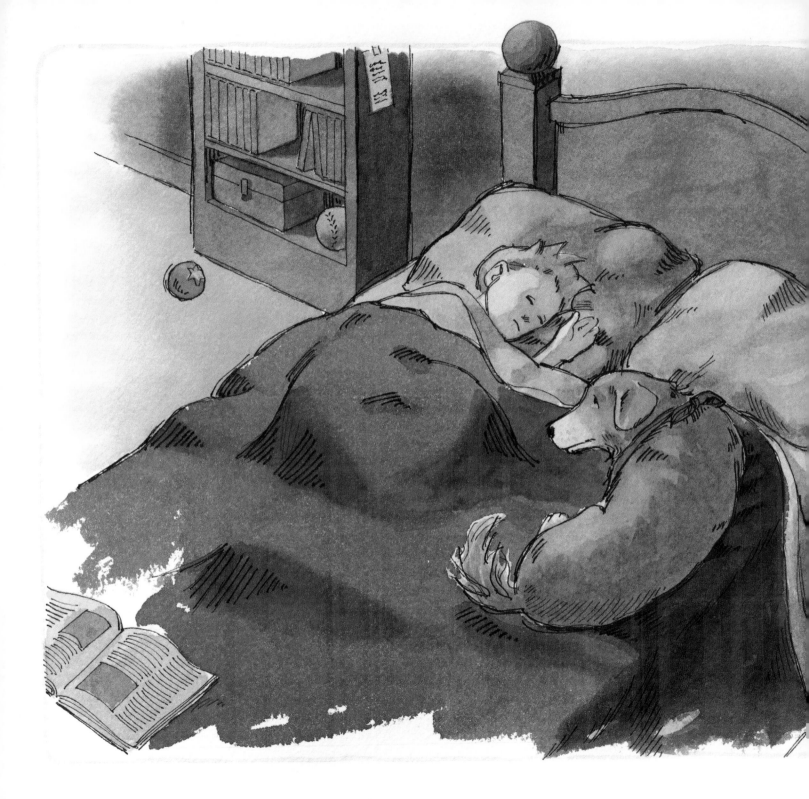

Often I'd live my days in a bed.

Matilda lay near me, real close to my head.

I sensed she had a deep love inside.

Never did she run away and hide.

She proved to be faithful, it made my head swirl

To think that Matilda beside me would curl

And snuggle even closer, so I let her be near.

A friend like Matilda made everything clear.

She showed me right up to the day that I died

Unconditional love from way down, deep inside.

I'm telling you this: Matilda showed me everyday

Feelings are important, and your pet will always stay.

When people find it tough to express the things they feel,

Remember friends like Matilda can be genuine and real.

I thank you, Matilda, you were there for me.

Know that I'm still living, only in eternity.

Someday all of you will get to see

An everlasting friendship, Matilda and me.

What did Matilda teach you about friendship?

How can you be a better friend, especially when someone is hurting or sick?

A friend is

What qualities are important in a friend?

The best thing about having a friend is